Dogs

German Shepherds

by Connie Colwell Miller

Consulting Editor: Gail Saunders-Smith, PhD

Consultant: Jennifer Zablotny, DVM
Member, American Veterinary Medical Association

Capstone
press
Mankato, Minnesota

Pebble Books are published by Capstone Press,
151 Good Counsel Drive, P.O. Box 669, Mankato, Minnesota 56002.
www.capstonepress.com

1 2 3 4 5 6 11 10 09 08 07 06

Library of Congress Cataloging-in-Publication Data
Miller, Connie Colwell, 1976–
    German shepherds / by Connie Colwell Miller.
        p. cm. —(Pebble Books. Dogs)
    Includes bibliographical references and index.
    ISBN-13: 978-0-7368-6327-8 (hardcover)
    ISBN-10: 0-7368-6327-3 (hardcover)
    1. German shepherd dog—Juvenile literature. I. Title. II. Series: Pebble Books.
Dogs.
SF429.G37M55 2007
 636.737—dc22   2005037363

Summary: Simple text and photographs present an introduction to the German
shepherd breed, its growth from puppy to adult, and pet care information.

Note to Parents and Teachers

The Dogs set supports national science standards related to life
science. This book describes and illustrates German shepherds.
The images support early readers in understanding the text. The
repetition of words and phrases helps early readers learn new
words. This book also introduces early readers to subject-specific
vocabulary words, which are defined in the Glossary section. Early
readers may need assistance to read some words and to use the
Table of Contents, Glossary, Read More, Internet Sites, and Index
sections of the book.

Table of Contents

4

Hard at Work

German shepherds are working dogs.

They can sniff, carry, pull, and lead.

They can search through rubble for people.

German shepherds guide
blind people safely
along streets.
A guide dog wears
a harness while it works.

8

From Puppy to Adult

German shepherd puppies
have floppy ears.
As the puppies grow
older, their ears stand up.

German shepherd puppies
have short coats.
Red or tan markings
color their black fur.

Adult German shepherds stand waist-high to people. They stretch their long bodies to run and play.

14

German shepherds have long faces like wolves. Their long, bushy tails wag back and forth.

German Shepherd Care

German shepherds must
have good food and
lots of water.
They need lots of energy
to work and play.

Owners should brush their German shepherds' coats throughout the year. The dogs shed the most fur in the spring.

German shepherds
make good pets
for active people.
They are smart, loyal, and
hard-working dogs.

Glossary

active—being able to exercise, play, and move around

bushy—thick and fluffy

coat—a dog's fur

harness—a set of leather straps worn by a working dog when it leads or pulls

loyal—faithful to a person

markings—a patch of color

shed—to fall out or lose a layer; German shepherds shed a thick layer of fur in the spring.

Read More

Fiedler, Julie. *German Shepherd Dogs.* Tough Dogs. New York: PowerKids, 2006.

Stone, Lynn M. *German Shepherds.* Eye to Eye with Dogs. Vero Beach, Fla.: Rourke, 2003.

Internet Sites

FactHound offers a safe, fun way to find Internet sites related to this book. All of the sites on FactHound have been researched by our staff.

Here's how:

1. Visit *www.facthound.com*
2. Choose your grade level.
3. Type in this book ID **0736863273** for age-appropriate sites. You may also browse subjects by clicking on letters, or by clicking on pictures and words.
4. Click on the **Fetch It** button.

FactHound will fetch the best sites for you!

Index

Word Count: 149
Grade: 1
Early-Intervention Level: 15

Editorial Credits
Heather Adamson, editor; Juliette Peters, set designer; Ted Williams, designer;
  Kelly Garvin, photo researcher/photo editor

Photo Credits
Capstone Press/Karon Dubke, 16, 18
Corbis/Reuters, 4
Lynn M. Stone, 14
Mark Raycroft Photography Inc., cover, 8, 10
Peter Arnold/BIOS, 6
Ron Kimball Stock/Ron Kimball, 1, 12, 20